My Point of View

My Point of View

Growing up on the Autism Spectrum

∞

Mark Hogan

To order additional copies of this book, contact:
Xlibris
1-800-455-039
www.Xlibris.com.au
Orders@Xlibris.com.au
721505

CONTENTS

This book is dedicated to the one I love, Leanne Hogan.

You have shown me the way.
You have helped me to see.
Without you, I would be less.
With you, I am more.
You are my guide and my inspiration.
Because of your persistence and love,
You have helped me see
Your beautiful mind's point of view.
I love you always. Mark.

INTRODUCTION

My family and friends affectionately know me as the ASD child whisperer. It is because I see what these kids see. I share their thoughts. I share their point of view. I understand them. I am the same as them. Connected. I am one of them. Mark Hogan

I was in trouble all of the time as a kid, and I couldn't understand why. It made me angry and argumentative. At school, I felt misunderstood by the teachers and the kids. And I didn't understand them either! I often felt left out, picked on, excluded, inferior. I felt frustrated. Sad. Depressed. I had low self-esteem. I was the target for the bullies. I was the butt of their jokes. At times, I was a nightmare for the adults… and I never intended to be any of that.

Now, as an adult, I am a loving, compassionate, kind man. I love my wife. I love my children. I love my family and my friends. I have feelings. Strong, deep feelings. Maybe even too strong. I feel disappointment. I feel love. I feel sadness. I feel joy. I hate bullies, and I hate cruelty to animals.

I have empathy. Loads of it.

And I have a conscience.

But at times, my behaviour does not clearly communicate this. I find it difficult to see from another person's perspective. And it is crystal clear to me that, at times, others don't understand my point of view.

I was diagnosed with Asperger Syndrome at the age of 31, after my son was diagnosed with autism. I experienced a myriad of emotions such as grief, sadness, and guilt during that period, but it also gave me a sense of relief. It offered me an explanation as to why my daily life was stressful, hence the reason why I wrote my first book, *'The key that unlocked the mystery."*

My view of the world is different to yours. Not wrong. Just different. Part of the reason I see things differently is my social understanding of situations.

I lack theory of mind.

There are mixed feelings about 'theory of mind' in the autism community. I understand this perspective. Much of the language used to define 'theory of mind' is confusing and offensive to some.

Some prefer to call it a lack of social understanding, a lack of connection, mind blindness, cognitive empathy, mentalising, and the list goes on.

Whatever you want to call it, is ok by me. But please, don't dismiss it altogether just because the terminology is insufficient, because if you dismiss it, you will never really understand me.

For me, Prof Simon Baron-Cohen's 'Theory of mind' means the following;

To be able to interpret another person's feelings, desires, needs, and intentions.

To be able to predict the outcome of an action made by me,

To be able to read another persons body language and have natural social interaction with others.

To be able to see things from another persons point of view.

To know when someone is been sarcastic.

To be able to put myself in another person's shoes and experience their feelings and thoughts in a situation.

For me, I believe lacking theory of mind is the biggest part of my ASD. This is also the most misunderstood part of autism spectrum disorder. I believe that if I did not lack theory of mind, I would be unlikely to get a diagnosis of ASD, because for me, this causes the majority of the issues I face.

Prior to my diagnosis, I had never heard of 'theory of mind'. So I certainly didn't know that I lacked it! This part of autism spectrum disorder was affecting my marriage, my job, and my relationship with my kids.

Understanding 'theory of mind' and accepting that I lack it, was a powerful revelation for me. It opened up opportunities for me to put strategies into place to improve my quality of life and this has been life-changing for me.

'Theory of mind' is said to be 'putting yourself in someone else's shoes', but it is much more profound than this.

My hope is to change the way people view 'theory of mind' and show them that people who have ASD do have feelings, they do feel empathy and that they do have a conscience.

To help you understand theory of mind, I have collated a group of true stories, real life accounts where lacking theory of mind has directly affected me (and the people around me!).

CHAPTER 1

CHILDHOOD– ENTER MY BRAIN

Being destructive

When I was a kid I had an obsession with helicopters. One year I wrote a letter to Santa to get me a helicopter, but instead I got a remote control car.

I liked the car and I had no problem with that, but my obsession with helicopters was strong and I needed one.

There was only one thing I could do and that was to make my own. I smashed my remote control car to get the motor out. Then I went about making my helicopter. I made a hole on the top of my Star Wars spaceship and stuck the motor half in it and half out.

Then I broke my sister's talking doll because I needed the on/off switch. I stripped the plastic back to expose the wire so I could twist the wire together to make a circuit. I got a 9v battery and secured that on with sticky tape and connected the wires to the battery.

I made a rotor blade out of two lollipop sticks, made a hole in it, and shoved that on the shaft of the motor. And there you have it. A helicopter!

I was so proud. I showed it to my mother. When she saw it, she went mad. I had no idea why. I had worked so hard to make something that I really wanted. I saved my parents money, so I thought I was doing them a favor, and instead, they went mad at me!

In the midst of this, my sister came out of her room, crying. She said that I broke her doll, and I said, "But you don't play with it, so it is a waste, and I needed a switch." I argued that I am getting more use out of it than she ever will. I couldn't understand why she was crying or why my parents were not happy. At the end of the day, I had a helicopter.

If Santa got me a helicopter in the first place then none of this would have happened, so it was not my fault. It was Santa's fault.

Getting into trouble for telling the truth!

I was about ten years old when my parents took me to visit an old family friend in the Irish countryside. We went in to her house and we all sat down to have a big old chat.

I was an observant child. Almost like a mini Sherlock Holmes. When it was time to have the tea and cake, I lost my appetite.

The lady offered me a cup of tea and cake and I said, "No thanks, Mrs. I'm grand." Then she offered me a glass of Coke, but I said "No" to that too. Then she offered me a glass of orange and I said, "No thanks." She said, "I know you like tea. You are like your father like that. You'll have a cup of tea won't yea." I said, "No thanks Mrs. I won't have anything. I'm grand." "Jaysus, I never met a young lad like you. Ya won't have tea. Ya won't have orange. Ya won't have coke. And ya won't even have cake. What will you have?"

"Can I have the biscuits that are in your cupboard up on the far right?" My mother went mad. "You can't say things like that, Mark! Asking people for things that are in their cupboard! They might be put away for a reason. You should take what's being offered to you. That's bad manners. Now apologize."

"Sorry Mrs." While I was watching everyone drinking tea and eating cake, I started feeling hungry. It was at that point I wanted to go home. They told me that I should have a cup of tea and some cake. The lady made me a cup of tea and I refused to drink it, and then they all wanted to know why I wouldn't have a cup of tea or a slice of cake or anything for that matter.

I felt under pressure at that stage. They were all there looking at me, waiting for an answer. You could have heard a pin drop. So I told them, and this is what I said. "The teacups are dirty. Only rinsed, not washed, and the same goes for the glasses. I don't want cake because you picked up the knife and wiped it on your dirty apron and this made my stomach turn."

My mother and father were not happy indeed and I think they were a little embarrassed. I didn't want to tell them all of this, but they insisted on knowing why I was refusing refreshment. What choice did I have? And to top it off, they had the nerve to be angry with me when they had started all of this!

I can see now that I could have told a 'white lie,' like *"I don't feel well,"* but back then I didn't have the skills or the theory of mind to know to do this.

The BMX story

I went everywhere on my BMX bike when I was a kid, but I didn't just ride my BMX to school or to the shops and back. I always took things to another level. If I wasn't down the River Barrow doing dare devil stunts at the riverside, I was probably up Mt Leinster in county Carlow, which is about 10 miles from my house, doing even more dangerous stuff. I nearly killed myself a couple of times.

I couldn't understand why my parents needed to know these things. I couldn't see from their point of view. I would be gone for hours. It wouldn't dawn on me that I should tell them where I was going and what time they should expect me back home. I could have had an accident or been seriously injured, but because I have a lack of theory of mind I never thought of any of these things, nor could I see why I should.

Time and time again I put myself at risk in some very dangerous situations. I know this now, but was unaware at the time. This is why you should always tell people where you are going and what time to expect you back. If you are not back, then they can go look for you. If you tell your parents what you are planning to do, they can advise you if it is safe or not, and if they are strongly advising you not to do something, they are probably right!

If you don't have a theory of mind you won't be able to see this so you are better off listening.

Cat and Dog (Please note –Some readers may find this story disturbing).

One day I was outside playing with the dog in our backyard. The cat from next door was sitting on the wall and started hissing at the dog. Suddenly, the dog started barking at the cat, and jumped up at the cat, but couldn't reach it. I stood back and watched what was going on, and I must say I didn't like it.

Every time the dog jumped up, the cat would swipe at the dog's nose. Just by chance, the dog got a hold of the cat, pulled it off the wall, and killed it instantly. When the dog was finished, I threw the cat back over the neighbour's wall.

About ten minutes later, the woman next door knocked on our front door, spoke to my mother for one minute, and left. My mother came out into the backyard to me and said, *"Mark, did you kill Murphy's cat?"* I said *"No."* My mother asked me again, *"Mark, did you kill Murphy's cat?"* I said, *"No."* My mother came right up close to me and said, *"Mark, I am going to ask you one last time. DID YOU KILL MURPHY"S CAT?"* *"No,"* I said. *"The dog killed the cat. I just threw it back over the wall where it came from."*

As an adult, I can see that I had a complete lack of theory of mind here.

*I can **now** see, a typical child would have been frightened at the dog's vicious attack on the cat. I know **now** that I should have run to tell my mother what was happening outside. My mother would have run out to stop the dog from attacking the cat, and may have saved its life. She would have taken the cat to the neighbour and explained the situation and apologized.*

It is important to note that there was no maliciousness on my part, in this scenario. Although my behaviour was clearly inappropriate, I was not deliberately participating in the cat's fate, or enjoying its demise.

At this early stage of my life, I wasn't able to envisage the impact of this situation for Mrs Murphy, my mother, or the poor cat!

Getting into trouble at school

One day, I was in class at primary school, and we were having a geography lesson. The kid sitting two rows in front of me wrapped an elastic band between his index finger and thumb to make a slingshot. He got a small piece of paper, rolled it up in a ball that he had moistened with his saliva, and catapulted it at me, and then snickered at me.

I immediately retaliated with a much bigger saliva induced ball and catapulted it back at him. That was fair, right? But he didn't even flinch. Then I got carried away thinking, "I'll teach you a lesson, ya moron." I burrowed down into my school bag and found a marble and I thought how good it would be to get him with that!

The kid sitting beside me started tapping my ankle with his foot. I didn't know what he was doing or why he was doing it. Then he dropped my book on the floor. I thought to myself, 'I'll get you later for that.'

At that point, I emerged out from under my desk like Rambo. I took aim and catapulted the marble at the kid two rows up and hit him in the ear.

The whole class erupted into laughter and suddenly I felt an eerie presence and the smell of Tweed behind me. That's when I realized I was in big trouble. The teacher was standing right there. She had been watching the whole time. I hadn't noticed. I was so focused on getting sweet revenge.

Afterwards, the kid that was sitting beside me told me that he had tried to warn me. "No you didn't!" I said. He explained that he kicked me in the ankle to warn me that the teacher was looking, then he threw my book on the ground so I would have an excuse for being under the desk for when the teacher came down.

Unfortunately, I could not read the signs. I thought that he kicked my ankle and threw my book just to be an ass.

As an adult, I can see that this behaviour is inappropriate and dangerous. I have learned some theory of mind. But as a child, I was overfocused on getting back at the other child. This is an example of tunnel vision.

Also, I couldn't predict the consequences of my actions. I could not see that the act that I was about to commit may

a) Cause serious injury, because although my intention was to get back at the boy, I didn't actually intend to cause serious bodily harm to the child. And

b), I couldn't predict that I might get into trouble.

The ability to see this was not there, and this is a clear example of no theory of mind.

The Class Clown

I was always the kid that the other kids would egg on to do something funny. I was the class clown. The teacher always said, "They are not laughing with you, they are laughing at you!"

I had trouble understanding what this meant because of my concrete way of thinking. From my point of view, try to imagine a comedian on a stage telling a joke. The joke is funny. We laugh at him because we think he is a funny man. We laugh at the joke because the joke he told was funny. So we are laughing at him and at the joke, If you were to laugh with him, wouldn't you have to be on the stage with him telling the joke and be part of it?

I suppose because I lack theory of mind I wasn't able to understand the teacher's point. That's why I never got it, and I remained the class clown.

I got bullied from time to time but somehow I found the strength to be funny and make people laugh. It cut down the bullying a bit. I thought to myself, "What's better? Getting bullied and being called a spastic and a retard or being the class clown and making people laugh." What do you think?

Playing soccer

Soccer was a big thing in primary school in Ireland. God I hated it. I wasn't good at it. I knew the rules but while playing the game I couldn't put them into practice, so I always got into trouble. I couldn't read the body language of anyone because I lack theory of mind.

Someone would shout, "Pass the ball" so I would. Then another kid would run up to me and say, "Are you stupid or something! Why did you pass the ball to him? He is not on our side." Then another kid would run up to me and say, "Don't mind him. Any time you get the ball kick it to me" You are on our side! You did good." That would make me feel better. Then I would get the ball again and the kid that was nice to me would ask for the ball so I would kick it to him and he would score a goal, pull his shirt over his head and run around with excitement. Then the other kid would run back to me with a couple of others and bash me because I had done it again.

Other times, when I got the ball it seemed like too many kids were there wanting the ball and it would get confusing for me. I couldn't read the signs. Everyone wanted me to do a different thing. I didn't want anyone to hurt me, so I would kick the ball up and run like hell. I really hated this game but the teachers made everyone play it.

Dancing

Irish dancing was compulsory in our school and all the kids looked forward to it. It was like a free class and everyone loved it. I hated it.

Why? …Because I could never read the signs of what I had to do next, so I was always a step behind trying to copy the girl. In the end she would drag me around like a rag doll. This always got me into trouble with the dance teacher because I was supposed to lead the girl but the girl ended up leading me.

The bike

One day my brother's friend came down to our house on his bike. At the time I had an obsession with bikes.

I used to take them apart and put them back together again. Sometimes there were parts left over, but they were probably not necessary anyway as the bike would still go perfectly without them.

I wheeled the bike out to the garage to have a better look at it. It was very dirty and the wheels were a bit stiff so I started to clean it up. It needed grease and oil so I got daddy's spanners and took the bike apart to clean it and give it a grease and oil. Then I put the bike back together again.

I decided to take it for a spin, just a little test drive. I took off up the driveway to gain speed to be able to go up the little hill at the end of the driveway that met the road, and then I cycled straight across the road.

At that exact moment, I could hear the sound of an air horn, the screeching of brakes, and the smell of burning rubber. I looked around, and then I felt the front wheel of the bike hit the wall across the road and I fell off.

The truck driver got out of his truck and started screaming at me. I didn't know what his problem was. My mother, my brother and his friend raced out to see what happened. They were like I was, probably wondering what all the commotion was about.

The truck driver told them that I was lucky to be alive, and that I just pulled out in front of him. They asked me if the truck knocked me off the bike. I said, "No, I just turned around to see what all the noise was, and that made me crash into the wall and fall off the bike and hurt myself, so I don't know what he is so upset about!"

Clearly I did not predict that a vehicle could be coming down the road at the same time I cycled out. I was just going for a quick ride. I did not anticipate getting hit by a truck! Lacking theory of mind makes me vulnerable to accidents because I just don't see the danger!

Special interest – Red Admiral Butterfly

One day I asked my mother if she would take me to the library because I wanted another book about butterflies. She said, "Oh yeah, the library. Like I have all the time in the world to go there." I said, "So what time are you going?" and she said, "Later." I thought, "Oh good," so I began telling my mother about the Red Admiral butterfly. I knew all about them and just loved watching them.

She was sweeping the floor at the time. She was doing a pretty good job of it but I would have done it better. Every now and again she would say 'ok' or 'that's good,' so to me that meant that she was really interested.

She went upstairs and started making the beds and picking up bits of paper off the floor, and she walked around picking up the toys and putting them away. I was explaining to her how the red admiral ate nettles and drank the sap from rotten fruit. Then she started vacuuming the carpets. I kept on telling her the story but I had to shout over the vacuum cleaner so she could hear me because I didn't want her to miss out on anything.

Then she went back downstairs and she started peeling the spuds, the carrots, and the onions, and chopped them up with the meat and put it all in a pot of water and turned on the gas. When she was finished all that, she put on a load of washing, then started washing the windows. I started telling her about the life cycle of the Red Admiral.

All of a sudden she stopped and looked at me and said, "Why don't you get out and play. I will call you in for your dinner when it's ready." I said, "When are we going to the library?" She said, "I was only codding yea. I'm not going today. I'll bring yea on Saturday."

It was clear that when I was a kid I lacked theory of mind or I would have picked up on the fact that my mother had no interest in hearing about the Red Admiral butterfly. And when someone says, "I'm going later", it might not mean that day, but perhaps tomorrow.

It has only been since I was diagnosed with Asperger Syndrome a few years ago as an adult, that I now understand a lot of the communication problems I had as a child. In fact, I couldn't read a situation as basic as a conversation between two people.

Dead people

Growing up, I had the experience of people dying, and going to wakes and funerals. Whenever I went to a wake or a funeral, I understood the boundaries and the rules of engagement between the deceased's immediate family and myself. I was always respectful and knew to keep quiet and just sit down and keep out of the way.

I was at the wake of an elderly gentleman who had obviously passed away but not everyone there seemed to be sad. Some people were laughing and appeared to be having a good time. Others were just sitting around talking about the football match, and others were howling like wild dogs.

I didn't really feel anything and didn't know what I should be feeling or doing. I didn't know what to say to anyone. I couldn't take part in the conversation about sport, nor did I know those people that well. They were old lads. I didn't know how to join in with the people having a laugh, nor did I know if I should try to join in and tell a dirty joke or something. I wasn't too sure if it was my place to hold someone's hand while they were crying, or hug someone because people were doing that. When you are young and have no theory of mind in this situation, you don't know what to do. You are lost and feel awkward. So I sat in a corner and kept quiet. After a while my father took me home and I was happy.

It was after this, I learned how people were feeling when they lost a loved one. Why they cried. Why other people laughed. Every person handles grief in their own way. Some cry until they can't cry any more. Some remember the good old days and have a laugh and celebrate the good times and good memories but sometimes it's too hard to do that because the heartache is too bad.

Some people think that people with autism spectrum disorder have no feelings or emotion but the fact is we do. They are so deep. Many people with ASD have a lot of emotional empathy but are low on cognitive empathy.

Inappropriate laughing

Some people think that people with autism spectrum disorder have no feelings or emotion, but I do. I have very deep, intense feelings. Maybe too deep.

Sometimes my emotions are hard to control and get mixed up. For example, when something awful has happened, I start to laugh uncontrollably, and people don't like me for it and start shouting at me for laughing and don't realize I can't help it.

One day, I was with my mother visiting someone in the hospital. While we were there, I saw a woman in a wheelchair that had suffered a stroke. I was very young and had very little self-control, and that combined with tunnel vision got me over focused on the woman's drooped face and the dribble pouring down her chin.

I couldn't stop looking at her disfigured face and I started laughing, totally unaware of my surroundings. It was like I forgot where I was, and I was totally oblivious to everyone looking at me.

Suddenly I felt the hand of my mother hit the back of my legs, leaving an unbelievable sting, which soon brought me back to my senses. She had to tell me that my actions were inappropriate and people's feelings were hurt. I never forgot that day. It was that lesson that my mother taught me, that helped me years later to be more aware of people's feelings and to act more appropriately.

The playground

When I was a kid in the playground, a boy named Luke came up to me and asked me to play with him. So I did. I was the type of kid that needed a leader, so I was happy to follow his lead and we played well together.

Another kid came over to play. He introduced himself as John. Luke started to play with John.

I didn't know what I should have been doing at that point when John came on the scene, but Luke automatically knew. The nonverbal communication or body language between them was natural.

At this point I stopped playing because I didn't know what to do. I couldn't pick up on the nonverbal communication that I could play with John too. I couldn't read the situation. This is because I lack theory of mind.

Their social interaction was a natural phenomenon to them, and a complete mystery to me.

This is why it is said that people with autism spectrum disorder lack theory of mind. This is a very common problem for a kid on the spectrum.

Friendships

I remember trying to make friends. Initially the other kids would make an effort. They would invite me to play various games and put a lot of time into teaching me the rules. Unfortunately, I simply could not read the social cues and I always stuffed up a game for everyone, which caused a lot of frustration.

In the end, I gave up trying, because I lost my confidence. I would get so stressed out that my eyesight became poor and everything looked as if a fog had suddenly come down and everything around me became blurry. White noise filled my head and I could feel pain in my neck and chest. Constant internal dialogues filled my head as I tried to anticipate interactions with others. I verbally role-played what others might ask me, and what I could say to respond. I would imagine in my head having conversations with everyone and it would make me feel very distressed. I would have to go lie down somewhere until it went away.

When I was a kid, it was hard to play because I had no idea of what the other kid's intentions were. The other kids got frustrated with me, because as a manner of speaking, they had to spell everything out to me. They knew this was not normal because they had other friends who were neuro-typical and didn't need to do it for them. Most times the result was that the child did not want to play with me any more.

As an adult, the problems are similar. A simple example is when I am folding sheets with my wife.

She literally has to tell me what direction she is going to fold so that I can follow her lead, and she always has to prompt me to follow her lead because I can't always read her mind, or her non verbal communication.

Group activity

Some kids on the spectrum do not cope with group activity.

Often children on the spectrum find it very difficult to break routine, since routine and predictability is what helps them cope with their everyday lives. They may feel uncomfortable in a group. They may feel too shy to contribute. They may become very argumentative and want things their way, causing raging outbursts, and possibly having it in for another student. I cannot stress enough; *kids with autistic spectrum disorder lack a theory of mind, they also have tunnel vision.*

If you must put students together in groups, try to pick the group carefully. You must work out each student's strength and put students who have different abilities together. That way you will have a balance.

Watch out for the student with ASD as he/she may have a great project but are not handing in their work because they are stuck on something technical and this will block them from being able to move forward. They get tunnel vision and need guidance to get around the obstacle, and only then will they be able to finish what they are doing.

Many people with Autism Spectrum Disorder try to control situations or do things independently because they are aware that they find it difficult to work with another person without getting frustrated and angry.

They are aware that they have a communication problem, so they prefer to do things their way. Children are the same. That's why some children with Autism Spectrum Disorder prefer to be alone, or, if they are playing with another kid, they will be in charge of the game and make the rules and everyone else has to try to guess what is going on.

Bullying

I got picked on a lot at school and if it wasn't physical it was mental. Sometimes mental abuse is so much more hurtful than physical abuse.

My earliest memory was grade one. Two boys from my grade came up to me and told me that they wanted to be my friend. I thought that would be really cool. They said, "Mark, let's go for a walk around the school." So I went with them. We came to the muddy puddle at the back of the school where the gutter was broken and all the rainwater from the roof accumulated in one spot and made a mess. The two boys tripped me up and I landed face down in the puddle. They threatened to beat me if I told on them. I took them literally and swore to never tell. When I returned to class, the teacher asked me what happened. I told her that I tripped while playing at the back of the school. She asked me if I knew I was not allowed to play at the back of the school. I said, "Yes Miss. We are not allowed to play at the back of the school." Then she asked if there was anyone else with me at the back of the school. I said, "No Miss. Only me." She asked why was I playing at the back of the school and I said, "I don't know Miss." I had to stand at the back of the class facing away from everybody.

The bullying went on for a while. You know, the usual schoolyard stuff until one day another kid came to the rescue. I don't know why he did because I'm not sure if we were friends or not, but for some reason he stood up for me. I always thought highly of him after that and I'll never forget the kindness. The boys never got physical with me after that day. I made friends with that kid, and it was through him I finally made connections with his friends, and once they got to know me, the bullying became less. There was just the odd snipe here and there, but the other lads soon stood up for me because I couldn't stand up for myself and they knew that. We were friends until we left secondary school and then we all drifted apart. It was nice and comforting to know that through thick and thin there were people watching out for me just the same.

I believe ASD kids need a mole in the class to tell the teacher in private what is happening in the playground so bullying can be dealt with quickly. If issues arise between students, an adult's perspective can be brought in, and any misunderstanding can be cleared immediately.

The Rat

I worked in one of the most prestigious horse racing establishments in Ireland when I was a lad years ago. I have many fond memories of some of Ireland's racing greats stabled in that yard, and the brilliant people who trained them.

One particular morning, I had just finished my last lot of the day when my boss approached me and asked me if I would work through lunch to get the yard cleaned up and looking immaculate. There was royalty visiting the stable to inspect their horses.

Naturally enough I said yes, and got straight to it. Three other lads stayed behind to groom the royal horses and everyone else went home. Lunch break was between one o'clock and four o'clock and the royal couple were coming at three o'clock.

While I was sweeping, a giant rat ran out of the feed room. It made me jump. It was as big as a cat, so I chased it down the yard and belted it over the head with a shovel. I tied a piece of string around its neck and hung it up in the hay barn for the dogs to play with and try to jump up and get. That kept the dogs busy while I carried on sweeping and getting the place spotless.

It was soon three o'clock and the royal couple arrived on time. I helped the three lads finish off getting the horses ready, so that they could lead them out and they could be presented beautifully. Things were going well.

The boss and the royal couple were making their way through the stables. Suddenly, my boss and the royal ladies' husband saw the rat hanging by its neck in the middle of the hay barn.

I was on the opposite end of the yard. The boss made eye contact with me. He had a strange look in his eyes and his face was as red as beetroot. He started making erratic hand gestures and pointing at me. I couldn't make out what he was trying to say, nor could I follow where he was pointing. He seemed to be pointing at the horse that just came back from a long spell in the paddocks. Surely he doesn't want me to present this horse. It's as fat as a fool! And it's covered in shit. They didn't even own that horse.

My boss couldn't contain himself any more and shouted, "Get that bloody rat out of here!" I quickly ran up and, with my very sharp knife, cut the rat down and quickly kicked it deep into the hay shed.

The lady turned around. She didn't see a thing and didn't realize what had happened. She asked what he was talking about. He replied "Sorry about that. It's just that I have a tremendous fear of rats and I thought I saw one, but it wasn't. It was only a cat. I am deeply sorry, my lady."

She just stared at him for a second and then looked at her husband, and then looked back at him and laughed and said, "I think you need to go to Specsavers". He just stood there with a smile and said nothing. Then they all carried on as if nothing had happened.

Being set up

When I was in school, I was open to all sorts of dangers, ranging from kids taking the piss, to kids getting physical with me. I didn't know when I was being set up for every one to have a laugh at my expense.

To be honest, I was feeling quite sad about the fact that this was happening to me. I just wanted a giant hole to open up and swallow me. I was so afraid of being attacked, I felt anxious constantly. I felt frightened every time I saw a group of boys walking towards me, because I thought they were going to beat me up. It wasn't always the case. I just could not read situations.

Sometimes a bunch of kids were just walking to the bike shed to get their bikes to ride home together. Other times, it was to pick on me. One time, a group of boys came up to me. The ringleader told a couple of the other boys to hold my arms and legs. He filled dirt into the hood of my jacket. He put the hood on my head and then pulled hard on the strings that tightened up the hood. He pulled it so tight that I could feel my hood tighten around my face. Then he tied lots of knots, making it almost impossible to see out from the hood. Dirt poured into my hair, falling down around my face and into my eyes and mouth, down my neck, stomach and back. I felt panicked and claustrophobic. Eventually I got the coat off and got my drink bottle out of my bag, rinsed my mouth and eyes, then shook the dirt out of my hair. When my dad picked me up and asked me what happened, I said, "Nothing happened. Just fooling around with the lads…" I never told him or my mother anything. I didn't want to panic them or see them upset.

There were girls at school that I was interested in. The boys asked me whom I liked, so I would tell them. Then one of them would say, "Would you like me to find out if she fancies you?" I would say yes. He would go, and come back with the other boys and say, "I just found out from one of the girls that she is mad for you. Go on, ask her out." So I walked over to her and asked her out. She said, "God, you're a big eejit," then she stood up and shouted over to the boys and said, "Get stuffed the lot of yeas". I walked away upset and thought to myself, "They did it again. I am so gullible. Why do I keep falling for their tricks?"

CHAPTER 2

ADOLESCENCE TO ADULTHOOD – CONFUSION AND DANGER

Pub rules

When I was eighteen, I went to a pub. It was on one of my first experiences, as I didn't go out much. I saw a nice looking girl. When I was sober I couldn't talk to girls. I don't know why. I guess it's because I'm shy.

So I had a couple of drinks to work up the courage to chat her up. I wandered over and sat down to talk to her. I asked her if she was into horses because I could talk a lot about that and luckily she was. So we were talking for a while and then a guy came up to us and said, "Are you ok, buddy?"

I was taken aback by this because he was calling me buddy and asked me if I was all right and I had never met him before. I said, "I'm fine. Thanks for asking". I turned around and carried on talking to the girl. He grabbed my arm and said, "You're a smart ass, aren't you?" I told him to go away and pushed him off me. He was invading my personal space and making me feel uncomfortable at this point. He pulled back his fist, then a friend of his jumped up and stood between us and said to him "Hey, leave him alone. He's not doing anything. He is only talking to her." Then he turned around to me and said, "I think you better go before he gets angry. That's his girlfriend you are talking to and he's fairly pissed."

I walked away not sure if I should have stayed and stood up to that guy. The girl didn't tell me she had a boyfriend. I wondered if he was the type of guy you hear about on the news that beats up their wives and girlfriends, or perhaps I just couldn't read the signs. I find this incredibly confusing.

I learned some time afterwards that when the guy said, "Are you ok, buddy?" it translates to, "That is my girlfriend, hands off". Now, how are you supposed to interpret that? Having no theory of mind doesn't allow you to read into that. Instead it makes you a vulnerable target, and I could have been bashed that night.

Growing up with no theory of mind is so disabling that, for me, it caused depression. Having no theory of mind really affects me in this world because I have no idea what people are thinking. I have no idea if I upset people. I could be in a dangerous situation and have no idea. I can't read faces or know if someone is lying to me. I can't tell if someone is being sarcastic or not, especially if I don't really know the person. I take everything literally. I put myself in danger when I went out to pubs because I can't read the signs, like when a bloke comes up to you and says something like, "Are you ok, buddy?"

She's not interested

I remember a year later I was in a pub having a few drinks, when I saw another girl sitting on her own and decided to chat her up. She seemed pleasant enough and I thought things were going well. Suddenly she said she needed to go to the bathroom. I said ok and waited for her to come back.

After 15 minutes, I decided to go look for her because I thought maybe something bad had happened to her. She might need help. I went to the toilet and came out and started walking back to my seat. That's when I saw her, sitting down with someone else.

I went over to her and said, "I thought I lost you." She explained that she had bumped into an old friend of hers and he bought her a drink and they started catching up on old times. I didn't feel comfortable with him there and I wasn't sure what was going on. I was a bit disappointed because I bought her a drink, so I pretended I saw someone I knew and excused myself.

This scenario happened to me several times after that. I figured out that when a girl says, *"I'm going to the bathroom,"* and they don't come back in 15 minutes, then that's it. They are not interested in me, and they are talking to someone else. It took a long time for me to cop on.

Talking to girls

I was not good at relationships at all. Girls would often stare at me and ask, "What are you looking at?" I would say, "Nothing" and look away and keep walking. I guess I could never find the courage to just go up and say, "Hi, how are you? What's your name?"

When I first took a keen interest in girls and eventually worked up the courage to ask one out, I failed miserably. It took me an hour to work up the courage. I didn't have a plan. I didn't really know what to say. I didn't want to ask any one for tips because I was paranoid that they would tell me the wrong thing, I started to think of movies I had seen recently, and lifted a few lines from there. I decided that's what I was going to say. So I walked up to the girl and I said this. "I really wish that you'd come home with me. You're so cute and I'm really good in bed, believe me. You smell good, too." That didn't go down too well. I got a slap in the face.

I thought to myself, "Thanks a bunch, Nicholas Cage," and that quote from the movie 'Leaving Las Vegas'.

I lacked confidence and theory of mind. I couldn't really tell if a girl was interested in listening to me or not until she would stop me and say, "Look, I am not interested ok". Then I would back off.

Another night, I worked up the confidence to talk to a girl. After a while, she started to yawn. I asked her a couple of times if she was tired, to which she replied, "No". So I carried on talking and thought it was going really well. Suddenly she interrupted me and said, "Hey, I just remembered I've got something really important to do. I have to go." After she left, I thought to myself, "It is just my luck to eventually meet someone and they have a crisis on their hands."

Over time, you can learn by experience what some signs and body language mean. Eventually it will come to you. Love eventually worked out in the end for me. I am now happily married with two beautiful children.

Things you shouldn't tell your mother

There are things that you just don't tell your mother. High up there on the list is sleeping with women, but I only found that out after I told her.

When I was young and stupid, I had been out drinking with a couple of friends at the local pub. I was a very shy, sociably awkward young man and didn't have much luck with the ladies. Later on in the night, we decided to go to a nightclub in the city. I didn't really want to go because it's too loud. I can't hear myself think, and I hate it when people bump into me. It makes me feel on edge.

Anyway, we were there and it was not going down too good for me. I just wanted to meet a girl. One of my mates pointed to a girl and said to me, "See that chick over there, all you have to do is buy her a couple of drinks and you're in", so I went over to her and bought her a drink. I think she came on to me straight away so I bought her a few more drinks. I wasn't much of a talker and struggled to make meaningful conversation so I asked her if we could leave, and we went back to her house.

I woke up the next day with a massive hangover and didn't know where I was. It was very early in the morning so I thought I should sneak out to get home. I felt I had been in that house before. There was something familiar about it, but I was too hung over to put my finger on it. Suddenly another woman came out from another bedroom and I recognized her immediately. I had picked her up last week and this was the house we came back to.

She asked me what I was doing here and how did I get in. I said that I was with her housemate. She said, "That's not my housemate, that's my mother!!" The girl's mother must have heard us talking and came out of her bedroom and asked what was going on, then the fight started, so I ran out as fast as I could. I walked into town and caught a bus home to my parent's house.

When I got home, my sister asked me where I had been. I told her the story. I thought it was quite funny but she didn't. She told me that Mammy was cross and worried, because I didn't tell her where I was going, or phone to tell her I wouldn't be home.

A few minutes later, my mother called us in for dinner, so we all sat down. It was very silent for a while. My mother said, "Where were you last night?" My sister kicked me in the leg under the table and gave me a strange intense look. I didn't know why she was acting this way. I was confused. I then proceeded to tell my mother what I did last night.

My sister started to cough loudly like when you drink some water and it goes down the wrong way, so I had to raise my voice louder to tell my mother the story. My mother didn't talk to me for the rest of the day. I assumed she was cool with it, but my sister said that she was far from cool. She told me she was disgusted in me, and what I had done was nothing to be proud of.

So that's another example of having no theory of mind. I just couldn't see or read any of the signs at that time of my life. As the years go by, I have learnt some, but often the hard way!

CHAPTER 3

RELATIONSHIPS – CHALLENGES AND LAUGHS

I just can't see the signs

The secret of a good marriage is communication. You don't have to be able to understand your woman. What man does! All you need to do is sit down and talk. Remember. Happy wife, happy life.

Before I was diagnosed with Asperger Syndrome, my wife and I had some communication issues. I, lacking theory of mind, was unable to read her signs. I was not able to pick up on the subtle hints when she was a little unhappy about something.

I often think back to when I was a boy, and I remember my father looking over at me saying, "A penny for your thoughts." He was always able to read me like a book. He always knew when I had something on my mind, and he was right.

I slowly learned to read when my mother and father were upset or tired. The fact is, I can learn some theory of mind, BUT the knowledge from one person doesn't transfer to another person because their body language is slightly different. Even though my wife's signs may have been crystal clear to typical folk, I couldn't read them because they were different from my parents, and my siblings.

For instance, I would be in the doorway dressing our daughter and my wife would be putting clothes away. She would come up to me with a load of washing in her hands, and she would have to say, "Please get out of my way. Can't you see I am trying to get into the room with these clothes?" If she didn't say that, I would ignore her and stay in the doorway and wouldn't move until I was finished dressing our child.

Other times, she would be doing housework and I would just follow her around talking to her. Sometimes she would hit me in the leg with the broom to move me, as I wouldn't think to move out of the way. This is all because I lack a theory of mind, and I cannot read the body language or her intentions. It used to drive her nuts!

I wouldn't think of moving into the bedroom out of the way and then helping her with the clothes to get it done faster. She has to ask me. All these issues build up. My wife now knows that she does have to ask me to move for example, because I can't anticipate or predict that she wants me to move. Knowing this has really helped both of us to manage these previous frustrations.

Food rules

My wife and I went down to visit her mother and father one day. We sat down and began to chat. Five minutes later, my mother-in-law got up to make tea for everyone. She brought in the tea and put a plate of biscuits in front of me and said, "Help yourself, Mark." I was feeling a little peckish so I ate the whole lot. Leanne had deep furrows on her forehead, and then a picture of a ploughed field entered my head. I was amused by it and smiled. She, on the other hand, was scrunching up her eyes. It looked like she had a headache. Poor darling.

Eventually Leanne said, "Mark! Those biscuits were for everyone!" I didn't realize they were for everyone, so I apologized. I couldn't see that the plate of biscuits were not mine, but were for everyone, and I could help myself to one or two and not the whole plate.

Luckily, the family understands me now and has a great laugh when they put food out. They offer the food around to everyone first, then say "There you go Mark, help yourself," with big smiley heads on them!

This shows that a lack of theory of mind is a phenomenon, which people with typical minds take for granted.

The plate of sandwiches

Here we go AGAIN!

Leanne, the kids, and I went down to Leanne's parents house for a cup of tea and a chat.

This time Leanne's mother put down a plate of egg sandwiches in front of me, and guess what? I was hungry so I ate the whole lot, and drank my tea and told Leanne's mother that they were the best egg sandwiches I ever had.

My father-in-law looked at me and said, "It's just a pity the rest of the family didn't get to taste them." I looked at him as if to say what you talking about? Didn't everyone else have a plate too? Then Leanne said, "You did it again Mark! The sandwiches on the plate were for everyone, not just you and you ate the whole lot." Whoops!

Meatloaf

I came home from work at the usual time. The kids were sitting at the table, with plates and cutlery in front of them. My wife said the dinner is ready. She went to the bathroom. I spy a plate of mini meatloaves under aluminum foil in the middle of the table so I guess it's my dinner.

I taste the first one and yuck, I don't like it so I put the whole lot in the bin. Leanne appears and sits down at the table. "Where are the meatloaves?" she asks. I said, "They tasted like shit so I put them in the bin." She said, "All of them?" And I look up from the table and say, "Yea, why? She said, "The whole plate wasn't for you, they were everyone's dinner." I said, "Well, how was I supposed to know. Anyway I saved the whole family from getting poisoned. You should be thanking me." Then Leanne started making something else for dinner because the kids were whining about being hungry. Leanne said to me, "You could be helping me get something else for the kids to eat, or give them a snack while they are waiting."

Because I lack a theory of mind I never stopped to think that maybe all the mini meatloaves were not mine so I shouldn't throw them out. And I should have automatically helped out to make a new dinner for everyone else, since I was the one that threw everyone's dinner in the bin.

It is this deficit that makes me a frustrating partner. I know now, for future reference, not to throw out the dinner, but the problem is this. New knowledge does not transfer on to other future scenarios, and that is part of the problem with theory of mind. For example, one day I kicked the dog. My mother came out and shouted, "Don't kick the dog!" and this was now a rule. However, a few weeks later, I kicked the cat. My mother went mad and said that she had told me not to do that. I said "No. You told me not to kick the dog and I didn't." I could not understand why I got into trouble again and thought she was being very unfair. Each lesson has to be taught individually and that is exasperating.

To be perfectly honest, about one month ago I actually ate a full plate of mini quiches that was supposed to be the family's dinner. Leanne has agreed not to cook anything mini again!

Bringing in the shopping

I was typing on the laptop one day. It was forty degrees outside and a cool twenty degrees inside. We have the best air conditioner. Quiet and efficient, just what you need. I was so comfortable and the words were flowing from my mind to the monitor like a stream to a river. I heard this noise outside the back door. It was my wife back from doing the weekly shopping, and she was making a triumphant effort in getting the shopping in out of the heat.

Her arms were loaded up with bags of shopping, from her wrists to her armpits. She did look funny. She was making her way from the garage, down the steps to the back door, and the keys were in her mouth. She was very red in the cheeks. I thought she might be feeling embarrassed, and wondered if she had stood in dog shit or something.

She stopped at the back door which is glass, and stood there looking at me. She had a face on her like a bull about to bust down a gate. Then she started twitching her head. She looked like she was trying to shoo a fly away. Then she put the bags down and opened the door and then brought in all the shopping.

She asked me what I was doing. I told her I was writing an article, and I proceeded to tell her what it was all about, quite excitedly, when she stopped me in my tracks. "Why didn't you open the door for me?" she said abruptly. I said, "You didn't ask me".

She went mad at me and said, "Couldn't you see that I was struggling and I wanted you to open the door! It was obvious that's what I wanted you to do!" I said, "Not really. You were just standing there shooing flies away with your head and flapping your arms, gangham style. Seriously, if you want help, just ask". She went ballistic.

Later, she apologized and said that it just feels like she is nagging the whole time. I said don't worry about it.

This is another example of having no theory of mind. My wife now knows to ask me if she needs help.

The air conditioner

After a long day's work in the 40C heat, I return home to our nice air-conditioned home, to find the house is hotter on the inside than the outside!

I went upstairs because I could hear the bath running so I knew my wife and kids were up there. The kids were in a cool bath. Leanne was running around in a lather of sweat. She looked at me and said frantically, "I can't find the remote control for the air conditioner. I have looked everywhere!"

With that, I reached up on top of the bedroom door and took it down and gave it to her. I said, "Well, you didn't look very hard." She went ape shit.

"Why was it up there? Why would you do that? You know I'm too short to reach all the way up there! I wouldn't even think of looking on top of a door of all places!" she fumed. "I put it up there because the kids were messing with it yesterday," I said, "and I didn't want them to get it because they can reach the holder."

She said, "You should have told me that you put it up there and I would have told you that's no good because I can't reach it and I would then tell you where you could put it so we both know where it is!"

As I said at the start, communication is the key.

PHOTO

Velcro

I had just finished tidying up the playroom. Next was the bathroom, but I thought I'd have a cup of tea first. Housework is thirsty work. Now, back to business. I always clear the floor first, then mop. But wait. What are these? I've never seen these two rolls of velcro before. What are these for and where do they go? I don't know.

I know what to do. I'll stuff them behind the handles of the vanity cupboard and I'll do something about it after. Now let's skip forward five hours and the guests have arrived. We are all sitting down talking then one of the guests goes to use the bathroom. On return, the guest (who is an interior designer!) asks Leanne what is going on with the handles of the vanity. Leanne says she has no idea and went to investigate. The two of them come out and ask me if I know anything about this. First I said no then I said, "OH yea, I put them there because I didn't know where they went." They all had a great laugh at my expense.

This is an example of a combination of having a bad short-term memory and no theory of mind.

My wife denies this vehemently (This nearly didn't make it into this book!)

When I'm talking about something I have an interest in, I can't tell if the person I am talking to is bored and has no interest in what I am talking about. They may have made several attempts to let me know without hurting my feelings, but I cannot read the signs.

When someone winks his or her eye at me, I often don't know what it means. Hand gestures confuse me because they are not consistent from person to person.

As I grow older, some of the more common signs are becoming familiar to me, but unfortunately not all of them. This is because they differ from person to person. For instance, the nonverbal signs between my wife and her sister.

Every woman has their own distinctive nonverbal gestures, unique to them. What I am saying is, the body language my wife puts out, is not the same body language as what another woman would put out. A sign my wife would make and I have learned what that means, might mean a different thing for another woman.

For instance, if my wife is sitting down and looks at me and lifts her leg up on the armrest, I interpret this as 'Do you want to come upstairs?'

So anyway, one day her sister was at our house and was sitting down on the couch talking to me about her job. All of a sudden she put her leg up on the armrest! I stopped mid sentence and felt shocked. I said to her, "Are you crazy? I'm married to your sister!"

She said, "What are you talking about? I said, "You put your leg on the armrest." She said, "I am just stretching my leg because I've got pins and needles from sitting on it!" "What's the problem?"

I was in the hot seat then. My wife and my sister in law demanded an explanation, so I explained. "When Leanne lifts her leg up on the armrest, she is feeling amorous, and giving me a message that she wants to go upstairs." My wife looked pale and said, "I do not! I have never done that!" I argued that she does. After a hilarious conversation, we worked out that I have been 'misreading' her action of putting her leg on the arm of the chair.

Then we all started laughing at the good of it. It goes to show how, after living with someone for years, you get to know them and their intentions, (or maybe not, as my wife insists!), but if you go out to work or a party or something, you find it so hard to read other peoples minds, their intentions and their body language!

CHAPTER 4

WORK – MORE CHALLENGES

My inability to see things from another point of view is profound.

As a person with Asperger syndrome, you spend your life trying to conform and fit in with neuro-typical people. It's not easy. It is a constant struggle and sometimes I say to myself, "Why bother?" It would be much easier to do what I want to and attend to my special interests, regardless of what they were at the time.

Having to comply with life's social rules of engagement, like having chats with co-workers and customers is tough for me. Sometimes, I have to listen to things I can't relate to, and they are waiting for feedback and sometimes I can't give any. But it's impolite not to listen to them. I have to be aware of my own non-verbal communication so that I don't show I am not interested in what they are talking about. I am always self-conscious, and this causes me to stress and get headaches.

I also have to try to remember to communicate to other people what I am doing, so that they know where I am. For example, "I'm going to the shop. I will be back in ten minutes." I used to just drive out the gate, leaving co-workers wondering what I am doing and how long I'm going to be. This takes a lot of energy to remember to do these things. It doesn't naturally occur to me to communicate these things to others.

There have been times when I was sad and emotional, and felt that the whole world was against me. It would be much easier to quit the rat race and not work, but I don't want to. I am proud of my achievements and I try not to let things get the better of me. I push myself and tell myself I can do it. Over time, I have worked hard and made some changes that have improved my quality of life. I feel proud because I am able to provide for my family. I give my children the best education I can afford. I bring them on overseas trips because I want them to have life experience and get to know their aunts, uncles, cousins and grandparents. I want for my wife and I to have a good life without having to struggle. I lead by example, and try to be the best role model and father that I can be. I have a beautiful wife and two beautiful children, whom I love very much and I wouldn't change that for the world.

Difficulty anticipating my work colleague's needs

There are situations at work to this day, where a lack of theory of mind affects my social interaction and my ability to work effectively with co-workers. This is a good example. One of the lads from work was asked to wrap a vanity basin in bubble wrap for a customer, because it didn't have a box. I was standing there talking to him while he was doing it. He said, "Aren't you going to help?" I said, "What do you want?" and he said, "The tape gun would be good." I said, "Oh sorry" then I got the tape gun and helped him tape up the bubble wrap.

I knew at that very moment, that was a lack of theory of mind, right there, because we both commented on it. It was an obvious situation where another person required assistance but had to request it, because I couldn't read the subtle non-verbal gesture he was making. He was standing there, struggling with a heavy object in his arms, trying to wrap it in bubble wrap and all he needed was for me to tape it up, and the job would be done. But no I just stand there, watching him struggle, and have no idea that I need to assist him. I just couldn't see it until it was pointed out. He had to ask.

I really do NOT understand why my wife likes sad movies

My wife likes to watch sad movies on the television and just sit through the whole movie crying. Why she puts herself through it, I do not know. Surely this kind of emotional release is reserved for funerals. I couldn't understand it, so I joined my wife one night and we watched the movie 'Pursuit Of Happyness,' (this is how happiness is spelt in the movie). She cried uncontrollably and I couldn't see why. I thought Will Smith did an excellent job.

Another program my wife sobs her heart out to, is "Find My Family." This is a reality T.V show that tracks down long lost relatives and reunites them with their families. Family reunions are filled with all sorts of emotions such as happiness, joy, and excitement. I understand why the people that it is happening to have these emotions, but I just can't see how anyone watching the show could go through the same emotion as if it is happening to them.

Different reactions and sensory issues.

People respond differently to situations. My wife has developed anaphylaxis and her tongue swells whenever she is really stressed. Many people who are watching this happening to another person would panic and wouldn't know what to do, because of its seriously life threatening nature.

Not me. I remain totally calm. I tell my wife to lie down. I get her epipen and administer the adrenaline. I note what time I inject it. I dial the emergency services and tell them the nature of the problem. I tell them her medical history and the medication she takes. I write it on a note pad and have it ready for the paramedics. I know from past experience that they will ask me these questions and usually she can't speak. I like to be organized. I turn on the front light so the paramedics can see the steps leading up to the front door. I get her Medicare card and her bag and phone and charger. When the ambulance comes, they take her to hospital and I go back to bed and sleep.

However, if anyone breaks a fingernail, I fall in a heap. It's like a phobia or something. Sensory issues play a huge part in a person's ability to cope with certain everyday situations because they can really turn you into a very dysfunctional person. To this day, the thought of bending my nails back can cause me to have a meltdown. Even writing about this is causing me to grimace.

When you compare the two scenarios, one is life threatening and the other is 'just' a broken nail. However the broken nail is a sensory issue for me, and this is one thing I cannot bear. It brings me to my knees.

For years I told my wife not to buy chicken wings because I don't like them, but that wasn't the case. So what does she do after ten years of telling her I don't like them? She dishes them up to me for dinner.

Here I am eating chicken wings. Because I am so sensitive to the feel of the grease and the sauce and I hate having sticky fingers, I can't bear to pick them up to eat them. I have no choice but to do this.

Since then, I bought food handling gloves and now I can enjoy all sorts of barbecue foods.

CHAPTER 5

MELTDOWNS – THE GOOD, THE BAD, AND THE UGLY

Meltdowns

I had plenty of meltdowns when I was a kid. Whenever I had a meltdown, I felt a tightening in my chest and a hot face and my heart beating so fast it could burst like tomato being thrown at a wall. I felt extremely upset and lost. So upset that I cannot hear what people are saying because every emotion that I have ever experienced in my life comes at once. Every muscle tightens up. I cannot process anything. Sometimes I cannot explain what's happening in the moment because I am experiencing such a huge sensory overload. I mean, can you imagine a situation where you are seven years old and you suffer from chiroptophobia (fear of bats) and you are in a cave and have come under attack by thousands of bats. This is what it is like for me to have a meltdown.

Can you imagine having a meltdown and you're screaming and carrying on, lying in the foetal position and then stop for an instant to quietly say to someone, "I am having a meltdown because of a sensory overload. I'm sorry. I do apologise but I will be with you shortly. Just help yourself to tea and biscuits and I'll get back to you when I am finished screaming in the foetal position?"

It just doesn't work like that. What actually happens is out of seemingly nowhere, a fully grown man (myself) starts screaming and drops to the ground, curled up in a ball and no one can get any sense out of me until I calm down. And then, because sometimes I can't talk about it, I have to write down what's wrong. Sometimes I can't even do that so no one knows what has just happened.

As a child having a melt down, sometimes it is even more difficult to explain why you are having a meltdown. Often you tell your parent what they want to hear because it's easier and you don't get hassled about it.

Here is a photo my wife took of me having an actual meltdown, after my wife suggested I go to a podiatrist to have my toenails cut. It was like it was happening to me...

Crown Casino

There are different ways I meltdown!

My wife and I went to the Crown Casino for our ninth wedding anniversary. The idea of it sounded good. We were both excited to be going and all I could think of was the movie 'Casino Royale.' I felt like James Bond – untouchable and ready for anything.

After we checked into the hotel, we wandered on down to the casino. My excitement turned into a feeling of high alert. I was trying to talk but nothing would come out. My wife was talking to me but I couldn't hear her. Every time I heard a bell or a buzzer, my head would turn in that direction. My inner channels and senses kept shutting down. It was like someone was using a radio wave signal blocker on my brain waves. It was like when my mobile phone doesn't have a good signal and it keeps dropping in and out.

The noise and the lights were too overstimulating for me. It was so bad that I just wanted to get out of there! I said, "Lets go." "But I haven't finished my drink, Mark!" said Leanne, surprised. "We are going. Let's go," I said. I was so disoriented that I didn't know my back to the hotel room. I begged my wife to show me the way out. I couldn't explain what was wrong with me. When we got to the room I still couldn't talk about it. I just ignored her and went to bed, despite her wanting answers.

The next morning I was feeling too bad to talk about it. I was so embarrassed. I had to just go and have a long shower until I was ready to come out and talk about it. After I explained to my wife what had happened and why I couldn't give her an explanation that night, she understood. I didn't have to say anymore.

If I wasn't diagnosed and that happened she would probably would not have understood me. Nor would I. And I'm not sure, but I think we wouldn't be together today.

So it was sensory overload that got me into trouble with the Mrs this time.

Crowds and social settings are overstimulating for my brain

Trying to filter out excess noise is not easy while trying to keep thoughts intact and keeping up a conversation. It is easy for me to lose track of what I am talking about.

One year, we went out to my work's Christmas party. It was at the Aquarium. I couldn't recognise anyone because they weren't in work clothes. It was only until they started talking that I gradually started putting the pieces together. Their faces were familiar but until they started talking, I had no idea of who they were or how I knew them. And, because I was in an unfamiliar place with background noise, it took me longer to recognise them. The noise, the lighting, the crowd, and the fish swimming around me were too overstimulating for me. Leanne actually introduced me to my boss at a Christmas party that year after working for him and seeing him every day for four years!

CHAPTER 6

PARENTING – A TAUGHT SKILL

Parenting skills needed to be taught to me. They did not come naturally. When our first-born child cried, I would stand over him, then would look over at Leanne and say, *"The baby is crying"*. Then I would look back at him, puzzled. Then I would say, *"He is getting louder."* I would get stressed and feel for him, and I would become more panicked. In a much louder voice, I would say, *"Leanne, what are you doing for God sake? Get over here, very lively!"* Leanne would respond, *"I'm coming! Why do I have to do everything myself? You are a parent too."* This just made me feel angry.

Eventually Leanne would have the bottle ready and Ben would be quiet and feed. Every time the baby cried, I would start to panic all over again, which was frustrating for Leanne. She had to teach me that, when the baby was crying, I could pick him up to comfort him, and this will help a lot and buy Leanne time to get a bottle ready.

Taking the baby for a walk in the pram was also a huge challenge for me. I would be pushing the pram and walk straight across driveways. There were a few near misses with cars backing out of driveways. Too many to be a coincidence.

I was not able to predict the potential (or real!) danger of cars driving into and backing out of driveways. This is a lack of theory of mind. I know that now, but back then, my wife and I didn't know that. She couldn't understand why that part of my mind was absent. Leanne had to teach me this skill. It took me a while to learn. Since diagnosis, I have virtually stopped arguing with Leanne. She has an excellent understanding of my condition. Having a partner that supports me, like Leanne does, makes it easier to tackle these issues, one problem at a time, and one behavior at a time.

Claire's finger

I was playing with the kids. Ben was six and Claire was three years old. There were a few spits of rain and, at the time, I was cooking a leg of lamb on the spit. I went into the garage to get the umbrella to put over the spit. It was only a very light shower and was over in a minute. I was just going to put the umbrella away when Claire wanted to know how it worked, so I showed her. Then she wanted to do it herself. She tried but she wasn't strong enough to press the button on the umbrella. I placed my thumb over hers and pressed down hard, squeezing her dainty little thumb. She screamed in pain. It brought her to tears. I got a shock. This happened because I lack theory of mind. It didn't occur to me that squeezing her thumb would hurt her. This didn't enter my head at all.

This was an accident. It won't happen again because I have taken a mental note. I felt so bad about it. If I had a theory of mind I would automatically avoid hurting my daughter.

It must be hard for someone with a theory of mind to try to understand what it is like to not have one. It really is a very invisible disability that's hard to fully understand. It makes it difficult for me to anticipate the consequences of my actions.

CHAPTER 7

CHANGE AND DISRUPTION – I HATE IT

Routine rules! Lunches

I like to have structure and predictability in my routine. It helps me cope with the day-to-day things at work. Because I lack theory of mind, it is important for me to have structure and routine so I can have some control of my life, and function as near normal as I possibly can.

This is why I have the same morning tea and lunch every day. I used to have banana sandwiches every day for a year until there was a hurricane that wiped out all of the banana plantations. Bananas were unavailable for ages, then the price of bananas went up and I couldn't afford to buy them. I couldn't have lunch until I found something else to replace the bananas, so I starved at work for weeks.

I finally found one particular ham I liked, so I had that ham for six months. One day the supermarket stopped selling it. I was back to square one again, and had no lunch.

My wife and I went into the supermarket to try all the hams. I didn't like any of them. All of the hams were slimy and wet and had an awful texture. Eventually we found a special one that I currently have now. Let's hope the shop where we get it from keeps stocking it.

I HATE CHANGE

Charity walk

Leanne said to me one day, "There is a charity walk next Sunday. Would you like to go?" I mumbled something along the lines of, "Yea, I don't know, maybe, maybe not." She said we should do it.

I don't like going to all these social things. There will be people everywhere. Dogs everywhere. I hate it. Leanne will be talking to people. There is going to be a number of unpredictable things happening and la de da de da.

Sunday came, and Leanne, Ben, Claire, and I went down to register for the 4 km walk. It was packed. We went up to the table, filled in the forms and paid the money. The lady gave us our green t-shirts. I put on mine over the one I was wearing. Leanne wanted to find a tree so she could dress herself and the kids. I said "put on the T shirt over the one you're wearing," and she said no. "The thing is just about to start and you are looking for a dressing room. We don't have time for this." She didn't listen so I waited for everyone to get ready. Leanne hands me all the clothes that they were wearing and asks me to put them in the car. I walked all the way back to the car, put them in the boot, made sure that all the doors were locked, then walked all the way back to the crowd to look for Leanne and the kids. Sometimes I am face-blind so I can't recognize them anywhere. I am getting angry because Leanne knows that I am face-blind but she decides to join the crowd and I can't find her.

I see a waving hand, and I recognize it is her. I keep my cool and I join them. We have to wait until we are given the instructions to line up and go. A minute later that happens, but just before that happens Leanne bumps into someone she knows (she knows a lot of people) and then asks me to start taking photos of us all. At that point I am thinking, "Look, they are trying to get people to line up to go out onto the road and you want me, against my will, to stop and take photos of people. They don't even look like they want their photo taken. Instead, I say to myself, *"Mark, you don't have theory of mind. You really can't tell what those folk are thinking, nor can you read their facial expression, so just do as she asks."*

We all start lining up and proceed to walk out onto the road. As that is happening, someone with a megaphone starts shouting at everyone to get moving. "Walk. Walk. Walk." As he made his way past Ben, Claire, and I, he shouted right in my ear as he addressed the crowd. Claire got a fright. Ben nearly had a meltdown because it was too loud and he is sensitive to noise.

I was really angry now. I was so bloody annoyed. This is one of the reasons I didn't want to be there. I knew how angry and frustrated it would get me. I said nothing, trying to be a good sport. After all, it was for charity.

We proceeded out the gate. Someone with a big box of fruit was standing there and shoving fruit in the kid's faces and mine. I tried to say no thanks, but Leanne said, "How lovely! That would be nice." I got angry again and said how bloody stupid that is. We are about to go on a 4 km walk and the last thing we should be doing is eating. We will get a pain in our guts. It was the most ridiculous thing I ever saw. No wonder there was paramedics on stand by.

We all started to walk and, of course Leanne and the kids were left carrying bananas and apples for a 4 km walk. People had dogs there. Our kids were uneasy. The whole pace was slow. Leanne, being the social one, started chatting to the woman beside her. Everyone was having a great big chat. People kept walking on my heels. People in front were too slow. It was loud. It was like I was surrounded by a swarm of bees and I just had to get away and find my own space.

I took off. I pushed through until I found a spot where there was a 10-metre gap between me and the people in front and the people at the back. I timed the people in front, and kept to that time so I wouldn't get any closer. I knew the people behind wouldn't catch up, so I was in a perfect spot. This was my strategy to help me not lose my temper. I am a peaceful person by nature. It was my way of been a good lad.

So there I am, counting in time the entire 4 km, and made my way back to the start. That's when I meet with the man I got introduced to at the start, where I took the photo of him, his wife, and his son. I wait with him and try my best to do some small talk but I am not good at it. I can't read if he wants to talk to me or not, so am getting really anxious waiting for Leanne because she is the talker and she knows everyone. This is so hard for me to do. Someone else comes up to the man and starts talking to him so now I can relax.

Ten minutes later, Leanne, the kids and the man's wife get back and straight away I was accused of running off and leaving her and the kids for dead. I said nothing and remained calm.

We decided to get a sausage and a drink at the BBQ stall. We joined the line to queue up. Leanne and the kids left the queue and started talking to someone else she recognized. The first thing that I thought of was she must not want a sausage or a drink because she left the queue. But since my diagnosis of ASD and discovering I lack a theory of mind, I said to myself, maybe I should get her and the kids a sausage and a drink. But the problem I am now faced with is, how do they want their sausages? Do they want onions or no onions? Do they want sauce or no sauce? Do they want coke or lemon or water? Do they want one or two sausages? I thought I would be in more trouble if I return with nothing, so I got four sausages three with sauce one without, no onions on any, two lemon and two coke. That was grand. I get back and Leanne tells me that I got too many drinks. I look at her and I give her a foul look and again say nothing. I am in trouble again. I am now so angry. All the anger and the hate of being at that event was so much that now I behave like an ass and I don't care because I didn't want to go in the first place. I only went to please her but that didn't happen and that angered me. I felt uncomfortable throughout the whole experience. I was made to do a whole day I didn't want to do. I was having a meltdown and at the same time I was feeling terribly bad about the way I was feeling because I don't want to feel this way.

This is the disabling side to Aspergers and autism that people don't always see. All they see is the bad behavior and the husband being an ass. But I don't want to be like that. I just want to be normal for once in my life but my brain won't allow me to do this. It just makes an ass out of me all the time and makes me feel so sad I want to cry. I can't win.

CHAPTER 8

COMMUNICATION – HITS AND MISSES

My Tried and Tested Conversation Tips

Conversations are very hard to enter into, and I needed a lot of practice to master this skill.

Some of us with autism spectrum disorder want to make friends, but it is not always easy because we may lack theory of mind or not have it at all. Many times, I have been shut out of conversations, or I have unknowingly pissed people off. Sometimes I can't tell if I am invited into a conversation or not, because I have difficulty reading situations and people.

I have learned over the years that the best approach is to listen in to the conversation without making it obvious. I don't stare at the people. I pretend to be doing something else like looking at messages on my phone. I make sure I know what the conversation is about, so if I do get a chance to enter the circle, what I have to say is relevant.

I wait for a break in conversation and then join in and try to bring in some insight into the conversation that makes people interested in what I have to say. It is really important to make sure my comment is relevant and on topic. Otherwise, if I start talking about something different, I am bringing confusion to the group. I try not to dominate the conversation, as this will piss people off.

If the topic changes and I don't feel comfortable, I make an excuse to leave the group. I say something like "Sorry guys, I just remembered I had to do something", then walk away.

When people are not interested in what I have to say, they may turn away from me, closing the circle. This is my cue to leave. When I leave, I do not storm off. I just take my phone out of my pocket, have a quick look, and walk away slowly, keeping control of my emotions.

CHAPTER 9

PERCEPTION – I DON'T SEE THINGS LIKE YOU DO

In the queue

We were at the airport lining up in the queue. We were in the line for ages and it just wasn't moving. I was whingeing to Leanne at how much I hate lining up. She said, "We are all in the same boat. Do you think everyone else here likes lining up in queues?"

So I looked around and pointed to a man with a big smiley head on him. He was having a great laugh. I said, "Look there! There is someone who is having a great laugh. He must love lining up!" She said, "He doesn't, Mark! He is just making the best of a bad situation, and talking with his friends."

I said, "You're wrong. I think he loves lining up. I reckon he is just lining up for the craic and having a great laugh. This is probably not even his line. I think he comes to the airport everyday and just lines up for the fun of it, and takes selfies on his phone, and posts it on Facebook to see how many likes he can get. He probably comes here every day to line up. I think he lets people get in front of him so they think they got one up on him, when in fact he is not really in the queue anyway. So the joke is on them, and when he gets to the front of the queue, he walks off and goes to the back of another queue having a great laugh. Just lining up for the craic." Leanne shook her head.

Next minute, the man leaves the queue. "I told you so! Look at that. He's going to the back of the queue!" I inform Leanne, to which she replies, "Mark, he is going to get a drink!"

Foul play

I remember watching the news as a kid. A story of a suspicious death was on and I remember the newsreader saying that the victim had met with foul play. Six months went by, and another person's life is taken by foul play. A few months pass, and then foul play strikes again, this time in a different county.

Life goes on as usual and the seasons come and go, just as my birthdays do. I am now getting ready for my first year of vocational school.

My mother has my uniform ready, and my lunch is in the fridge. Dad is watching the six o'clock news and another body is found, and he has also met with foul play.

I looked at my dad and said, "The cops need to catch this dude. It's scary to think that there is someone out there going around killing people, willy-nilly. He has been on the run for years! He must be very quick and clever to get away with killing all of these people and not leave a shred of evidence. Why haven't the police caught him yet? Has anyone ever seen him? Why are people constantly meeting with him? Don't they know all he wants to do is kill?. This time he chose a woman, so it doesn't seem to matter to him if his victims are male or female. He just likes the thrill of the kill. This is a very evil man indeed. He has to be stopped. Why can't the police find him? It really baffles me. This Foul Play dude is one slippery criminal."

Then my father said this. "Foul play is not a person! All this means is their deaths were suspicious, not an accident, but probably murder".

I took everything literally, so I thought Foul Play was a person. I felt really stupid and then angry that police and newsreaders would play with words like that and lead me up the garden path.

Metaphors

I used to think people were talking in code when they wanted to say something that they didn't want me to hear but couldn't wait until I was gone. This used to get me so paranoid. I used to think they were talking about me.

It wasn't until I was thirty-five years old before I realized this was not the case. People use metaphors in conversations and I never understood this. When people are talking, they assume everyone in the conversation understands and, in most cases, everyone does so it's never an issue. People are not going to stop mid conversation and say, "Oh shit. Sorry! I just used a metaphor. I hope everyone understands, but it just rolled off my tongue. Oh good. You do! "And then carry on talking.

I wish I were born with a theory of mind. Then I wouldn't have had to go through my whole life clueless to my social surroundings and having to feel my way around this speaking world. Its almost like being dropped off in Tokyo city and having to make your way on foot, to Kyushu which is 1,210 km away. It's not impossible but a big ask all the same.

CHAPTER 10

LITERAL THINKING – LEADS ME UP THE GARDEN PATH!

Who's Harvey Norman!!!

Leanne and I had been dating for about four months. There was one particular day I found myself in a deep, dark mood. I was not amused. Well, as a matter of fact, I was very upset. She had told me how much she loved this other man and, to make matters worse, she stood there, in the kitchen, caressing the fridge and told me that she got it from Harvey Norman. So I furiously asked her, "What else did you get from Harvey Norman?" She said "Oh, I got this from Harvey Norman (pointing to the dish washer). I got the freezer from Harvey Norman, I got the microwave from Harvey Norman and I got the washing machine from Harvey Norman."

I felt my frown grow deep, and my blood boil. How can I compete with this rich bastard that keeps giving her such good presents? And she just stands there with a big smiley head on her, rubbing it in, and waiting for me to be happy for her. How can I be? I mean, how can I compete with that? Seriously. I think she has some cheek. I decide to pack my bags to go back to Ireland. I don't want to. I have come all this way for the love of my life. I don't want to give up on us, but I really don't know what to do to show her I'm better than him.

At this stage, I haven't spoke to Leanne all day and she said, "Clearly this relationship has run its course. I am getting tired of the silent treatment, so before we call it quits, is there anything you would like to say?" I wanted to fight for her, so I look her in the eye and said, "Who's Harvey Norman".

"What?" she said. I said, "Who is Harvey Norman?"

"Is that what this is about?" she asked. I said, "Yes." She laughed for ten minutes before she was able to say anything. I thought she was being extremely rude. Then, as she wiped away tears, she told me Harvey Norman is a shop that sells white goods, electrical goods, and furniture. She continued to laugh for the rest of the day and I felt a sigh of relief.

Later that evening, we sat down to watch some television. I stood up and placed my hand on the television said jokingly, "I suppose you got this from Harvey Norman too." She said, "No. I got that from Dick Smith." Well, she said you should have seen the look on my face. It was priceless. (He sells electrical goods too!)

CHAPTER 11

RULES – MY WAY OR THE HIGHWAY

Driving

A person once said to me, if you lack a theory of mind then how do you go at driving a car. I said, "First of all, I got ninety-eight percent in my driving license theory test. Now I'll tell you a practical example. I am at a yield give way sign and a car is approaching slowly on my right and doesn't have an indicator on to make a left-turn. Also, some people have their indicators on and don't realize it and don't turn, so that makes it hard to know their intentions. I have learned one thing and it is this. *Most* of the time when a person is in charge of a motor vehicle, they will do the right thing by other motorists and stick to the rules of driving safely on the road. However, you will get the odd one that will not obey the rules and are a danger to other road users. So when you throw this into the equation, you have to factor this in as well."

I can't predict what people intend to do so I wait until that person makes their move first. I wait until they make their move before I proceed to drive out onto the road so long as it is clear.

As long as people obey the rules of safe driving there shouldn't be a problem. By nature of a person on the spectrum, that person will be a stickler for the rules and in general will make a good driver.

The green man – crossing the road

The rules of a pedestrian crossing are simple. When you see the green man, you cross the road. When he is flashing red, you hurry up and finish the crossing, because this is a warning that he is about to be red, and when he is red, you don't cross the road.

My wife and I have issues crossing the road. When we have to cross the road, we do the usual thing everyone does. We push the button and wait for the green man. He lights up and I bolt across the road and leave her for dead.

So, I am at the other side of the road looking at her casually walking across the road, and, as she does that, I start panicking because the green man is no longer green. It is now flashing red, warning that it is about to turn solid red any second now, and I can see cars inching forward! I can hear engines revving. They are about to take off and that's when I shout at my wife and tell her to hurry up and start running. When she finally gets across, she goes mad at me for yelling at her. I have no idea why she has a go at me.

She says I should walk with her, instead of running off and leaving her on her own. I say, "No way." I like to get across the road with time to spare, because I might run out of time and everyone will start driving again and knock me down or abuse me. I hate people crossing the road when they should not. It makes me angry because they are not following the rules. They think that they are above the law or something. I don't like that.

CHAPTER 12

FINAL WORDS – OR ARE THEY?

Family day

I was at a family day at my son's school. It was fairly interesting, I met a lot of the other parents, which was cool, but there was one child that caught my attention. He was giving the two teachers that were guarding the door to the playground a hard time. They were also guarding the tea, sugar, and coffee. He would run up to the table with the tea bags, coffee and sugar and swiftly knock them to the floor. While the teachers were picking up tea bags, he would make a run for the door as people were coming in. He couldn't reach the handle because it was far too high, so he had to wait for his chance.

When there was no one coming in or out, he was running around having fun. But at the same time, he was watching the door. As soon as he spotted someone walking towards the door, he would run back up to the tea, coffee and sugar and knock them over lightning fast, to cause a distraction, then curl up into a ball and roll through the teachers legs and bolt out the door.

I thought this was clever and funny. I loved it. I went out to watch him just in case he was not using the play equipment appropriately. But he did. After a while, people were starting to go home and his mother came out with a baby and a toddler in her arms. His mother wanted him to stop and go home with her. One of the teachers tried to catch him. He was running around the schoolyard having a laugh but with no theory of mind. I said I would get him and help bring him to the car.

I approached him. As he went to run past, I knelt down and opened my arms and called his name and he ran into them. I held his hand and said it was finished and it's time to go home. With that, I stood up and he walked quietly by my side out the gate over to the car. I helped him into the car seat and buckled him up. His mother and the teachers looked on in amazement at how peaceful that little boy went with me to the car, and didn't even try to play up once.

Some people can't see past the autism but I assure you beyond autism, is a beautiful, clever person just like everyone else. People on the autistic spectrum understand everything you say, so be aware.

CONCLUSION

I was born with no script. I was born with an empty manuscript of which I need to fill in myself, day by day. I lack theory of mind, so making sense of this world can be an enormous challenge for me.

Every single incident in my life is captured and stored in this internal manuscript that are my memories.

Fortunately, I can look back on it and use it as a reference. It's like a logbook, ready to be used as a guide in any current situation. My childhood memories are so clear.

I refer to my memories in the same way teachers refer to their manual to help them out in a teaching/learning situation. I use them as a reference guide to go about my daily life.

I rely on these memories to help shape and build my future.

Everything I learned came from my parents, siblings, peers, teachers, aunts, uncles and neighbours. I am grateful to all of them for showing me the way.

I hope you have enjoyed reading my book. I hope that I have helped you to understand theory of mind in layman's terms, through sharing my life experiences.

If you are a person with ASD, my book may help you to explain your way of thinking to your social network of family, friends, and colleagues.

My behaviour can bamboozle even those who are closest to me, but I *always* have a reason for my thoughts and my actions. Often people just can't see from my point of view.

Lightning Source UK Ltd.
Milton Keynes UK
UKOW04f1117050917
308617UK00002B/661/P